Copyright Page:

Mama Claus and the Orphanage
Copyright@2024 Albert Kirkland

All rights reserved. No portion of this publication may be reproduced, distributed, or transmitted in any form or by any means, including photocopying, recording, or other electronic or mechanical methods, without the prior written permission of the publisher.

Book Cover and Illustrations by: Urusa Zeeshan
Printed in United States of America: First printing, 2024
Library of Congress Registration Number: TXu2439568
ISBN: 979-8-9891723-9-9

Dedication Page:

This book is dedicated to and inspired by my mother, Sarah Nelson. Every Christmas, I watched her make ends meet and give from her heart to her own children and others. She has taught disabled children and given to her community in ways too numerous to count. She treats every child as if they were her own, and so many love her for it. Her love, compassion, kindness, and selflessness make her truly special. And of course, she bakes the best sweet potato pies in the world. Thank you for everything, Mama Claus! This book is also dedicated to the best two sisters in the world, Sheneece and Tomekia Kirkland, who remind me so much of our mother. Love you both forever!

Once upon a time, in the small town of Sumter, there was an orphanage with 15 adorable children who had lived there for two years without parents. Just before Christmas, they met a new cafeteria worker who would change their lives forever!

"Good morning, children," said Mr. Johnson, the head of the orphanage, as they entered the cafeteria for breakfast. "I would like you to meet our new cook, Mrs. Nelson."

"Hi, Mrs. Nelson," they all replied grumpily.

Carter whispered to his friend Kania, "Another grown-up who doesn't care about us. Mr. Johnson acts like he cares, but never does anything for us unless people are watching."

Kania giggled, but Mr. Johnson heard her.

"Is there something you'd like to say, Kania?" he asked.

"No, sir," Kania replied.

"Okay children, hurry up and eat your breakfast. Then it's off to school," said Mr. Johnson.

Mrs. Nelson noticed the sad mood on the children's faces, the hopeless orphanage, and the lack of Christmas spirit. The building felt like a box without joy, cheerfulness, or love. As Carter went through the breakfast line, she overheard him telling Kania, "We eat the same thing daily. Mr. Johnson hires more workers, but won't even get us a Christmas tree!"

Kania. replied, "Well, Mrs. Nelson seems nice."

Carter sighed, "Yeah, but grown-ups are all the same."

Mrs. Nelson's skin glowed like sweet honey that never seemed to age. Grey and white hair that looked like a newspaper page. Her bright eyes twinkled like lit Christmas trees on Christmas Eve, with rosy cheeks, like new flowers in the spring. Her body was shaped like a soft cupcake, with a smile that could make anyone love, instead of hate. She brought warmth and joy wherever she would roam, making every child feel special and at home.

"Good morning, children," said Mrs. Nelson. "I wish you all a good day at school. Tonight, I'll make some homemade cookies for you all!" The kids were shocked and excited.

"Really?" said Kania. "No one ever made us cookies."

Mr. Johnson quickly came over. "Mrs. Nelson, we do not have food supplies for cookies," he said firmly.

The children's excitement faded. Mrs. Nelson smiled kindly. "No worries, Mr. Johnson. I'll use my own supplies."

He frowned, but said, "Well, alright, since it's your own food," and returned to his office. The children cheered, "Thank you so much!"

"Off to school now, and I'll see you tonight," said Mrs. Nelson.

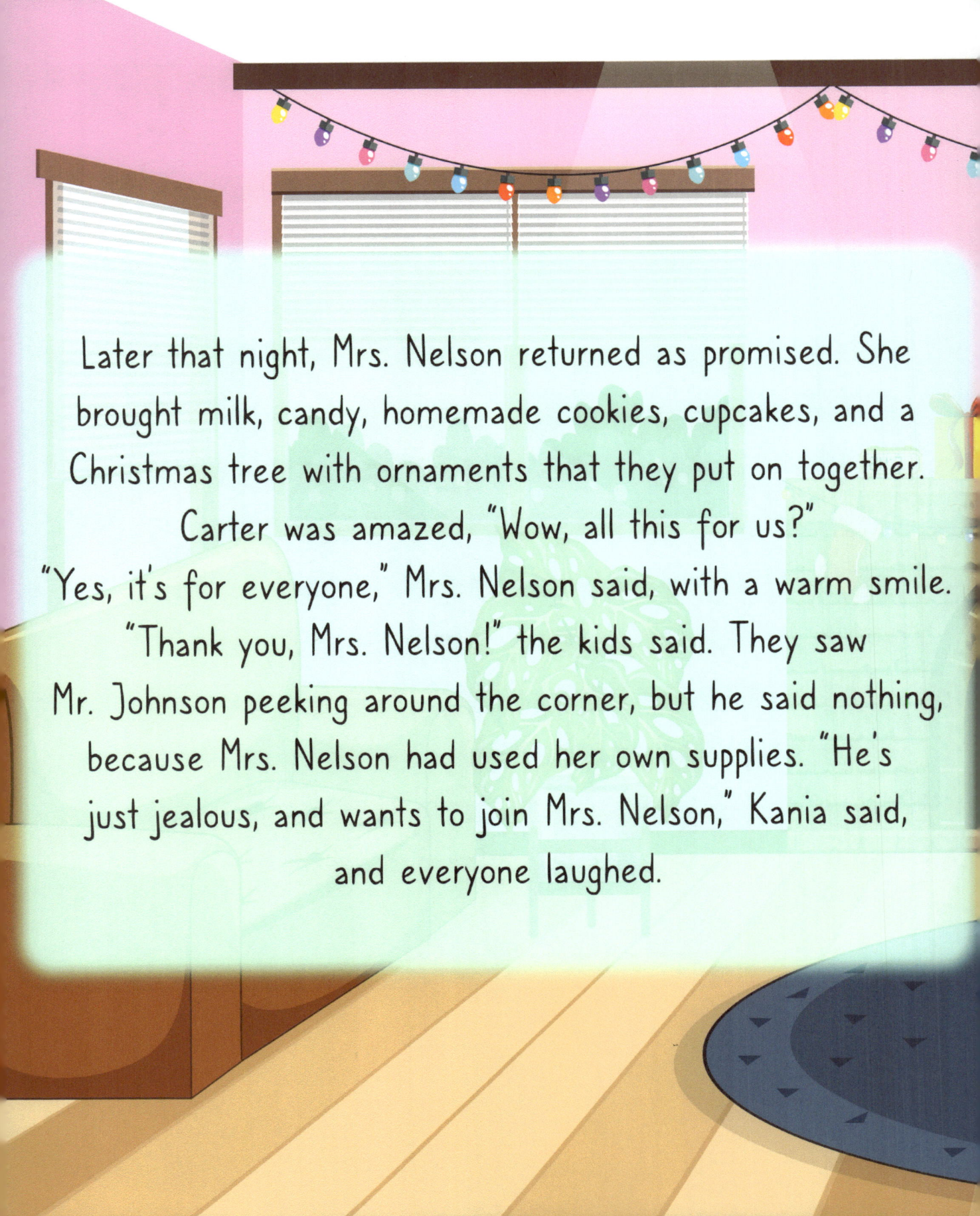

Later that night, Mrs. Nelson returned as promised. She brought milk, candy, homemade cookies, cupcakes, and a Christmas tree with ornaments that they put on together. Carter was amazed, "Wow, all this for us?"
"Yes, it's for everyone," Mrs. Nelson said, with a warm smile.
"Thank you, Mrs. Nelson!" the kids said. They saw Mr. Johnson peeking around the corner, but he said nothing, because Mrs. Nelson had used her own supplies. "He's just jealous, and wants to join Mrs. Nelson," Kania said, and everyone laughed.

"Gather around, children, so that I can tell you a story," said Mrs. Nelson. She shared a story about a woman named Mama Claus, that helped children at Christmas in her own special way. She would just show up to different places and share her warmth, kindness, and love for children who felt forgotten. "We've never heard that story before!" the children exclaimed.

"I know, that's why I'm telling it to you now, so that you can tell your children someday," Mrs. Nelson replied with a grandma smile on her face.

"That was a great story, and the cookies were delicious!" the children said excitedly. They clapped and begged for another story. "This is the only one for tonight, but come sit on my lap and tell me what you want for Christmas," Mrs. Nelson said. She hugged them, and they all started crying tears of joy.

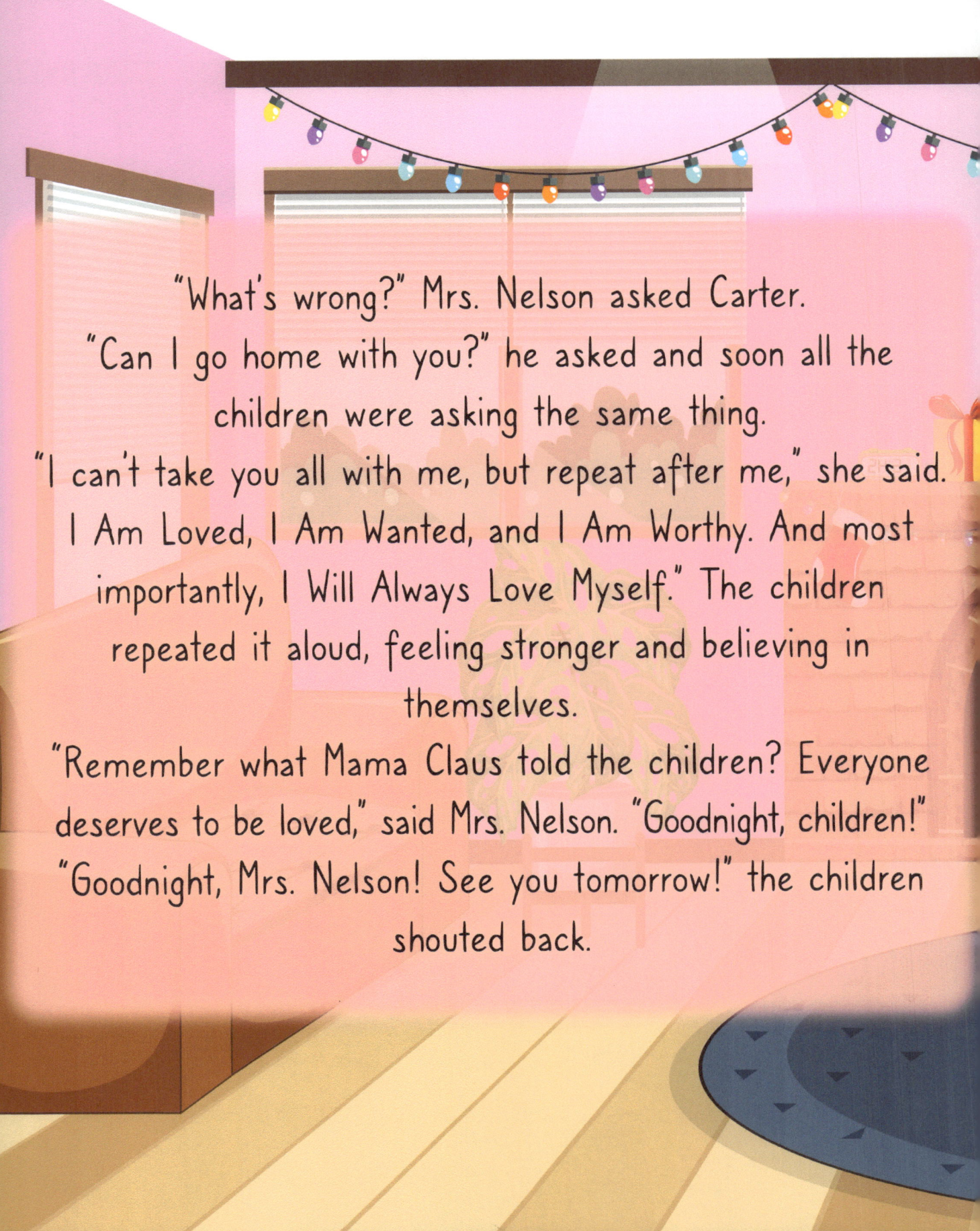

"What's wrong?" Mrs. Nelson asked Carter.
"Can I go home with you?" he asked and soon all the children were asking the same thing.
"I can't take you all with me, but repeat after me," she said. I Am Loved, I Am Wanted, and I Am Worthy. And most importantly, I Will Always Love Myself." The children repeated it aloud, feeling stronger and believing in themselves.
"Remember what Mama Claus told the children? Everyone deserves to be loved," said Mrs. Nelson. "Goodnight, children!"
"Goodnight, Mrs. Nelson! See you tomorrow!" the children shouted back.

A couple of days later, Mr. Johnson approached Mrs. Nelson. "You know it's not good to spoil these children. They'll expect this treatment all the time," he said.

Mrs. Nelson smiled, "What's wrong with feeling loved? Why shouldn't they be treated like this always?" Mr. Johnson had no reply, so he nodded and returned to his office.

The children's faces were more excited and cheerful than ever as they ate breakfast. "Off to school you go, and remember to repeat everything I taught you last night," said Mrs. Nelson.
"Will you tell us a story tonight?" Kania asked.
"Yes, I will," Mrs. Nelson replied with a grandma smile on her face.

Just like the first night, Mrs. Nelson brought milk, cupcakes, cookies, and some of her homemade sweet potato pie. She also brought gifts for the children to put under the Christmas tree. "Wow!" said the children. "You must really love us," Carter said.

"I surely do," Mrs. Nelson replied with that warm and sweet grandma smile.

"Will tonight's story be about Mama Claus?" Carter asked.

"Tonight story is about Mama Claus," said Mrs. Nelson. Kania asked, "Mrs. Nelson, do you know Mama Claus? You know a lot of stories about her."

Mrs. Nelson replied, "Yes, and she keeps a naughty or nice list just like Santa. So you all better be on your best behavior. Now, let's repeat what I told you last night: I Am Loved, I Am Wanted, I Am Worthy, and I Will Always Love Myself!"

As the children lay down to sleep, Kania whispered to Carter, "Do you think Mama Claus is real? Do you think Mrs. Nelson is Mama Claus?"

Carter replied, "No, if Mama Claus was real, she wouldn't come here. Nevertheless, I still love Mrs. Nelson; she's the best."
"Well, she acts and talks like Mama Claus in the story and made us a sweet potato pie just like Mama Claus did," Kania said as they fell asleep.

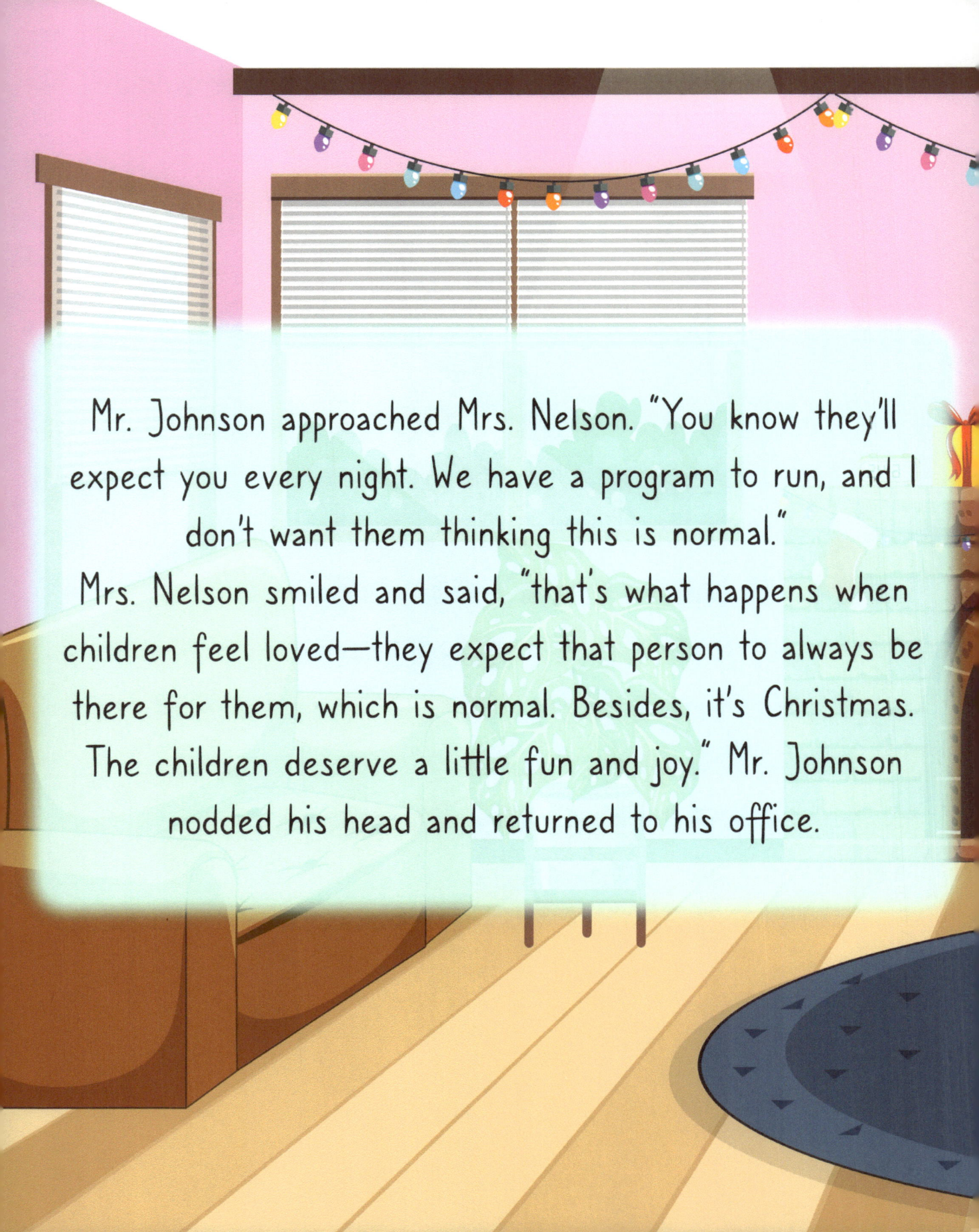

Mr. Johnson approached Mrs. Nelson. "You know they'll expect you every night. We have a program to run, and I don't want them thinking this is normal."

Mrs. Nelson smiled and said, "that's what happens when children feel loved—they expect that person to always be there for them, which is normal. Besides, it's Christmas. The children deserve a little fun and joy." Mr. Johnson nodded his head and returned to his office.

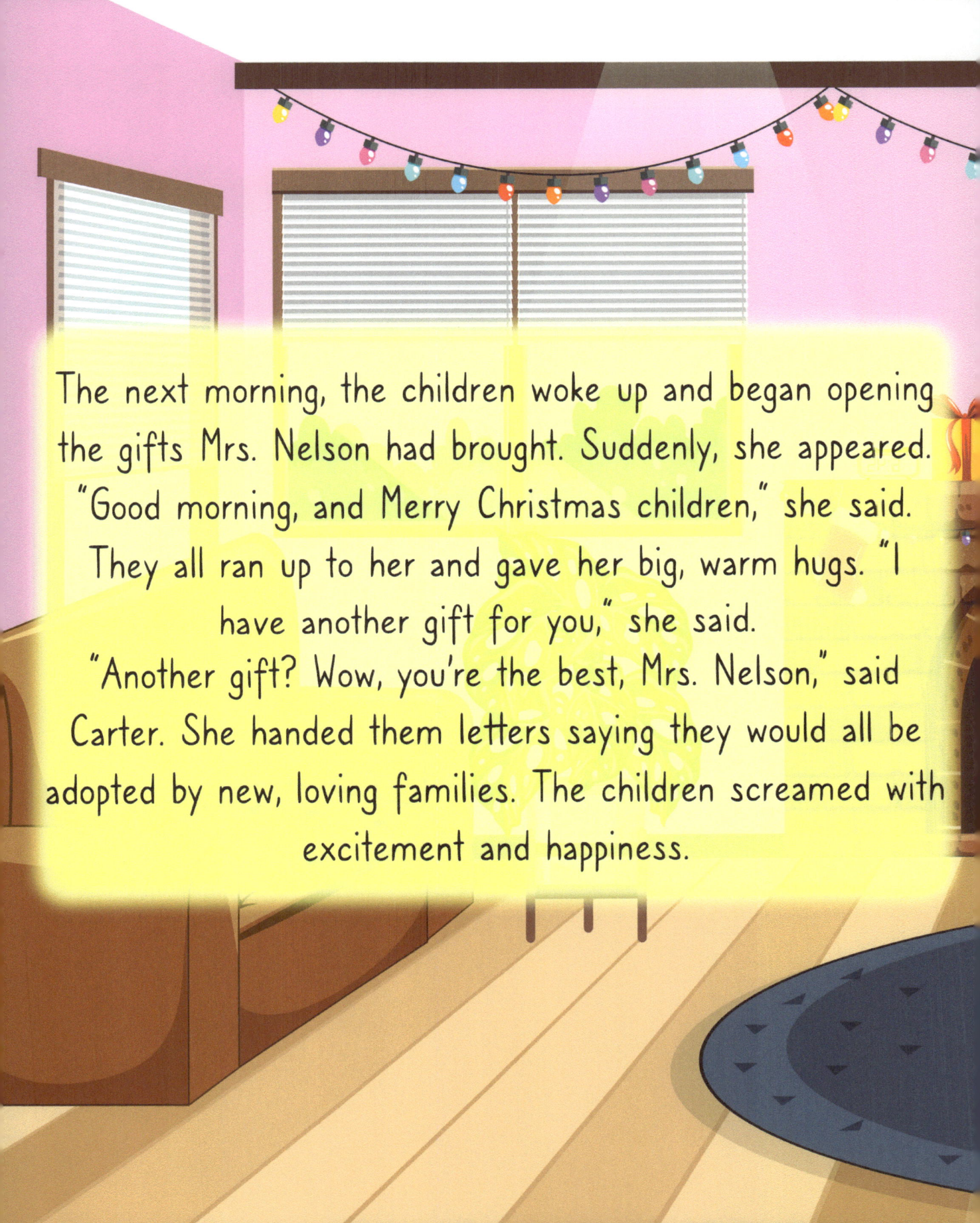

The next morning, the children woke up and began opening the gifts Mrs. Nelson had brought. Suddenly, she appeared. "Good morning, and Merry Christmas children," she said. They all ran up to her and gave her big, warm hugs. "I have another gift for you," she said.

"Another gift? Wow, you're the best, Mrs. Nelson," said Carter. She handed them letters saying they would all be adopted by new, loving families. The children screamed with excitement and happiness.

Kania whispered to Carter, "I told you she was Mama Claus." They giggled and laughed. "Yes, she is Mama Claus, and miracles truly do happen for kids like us," said Carter with a big smile on his face.

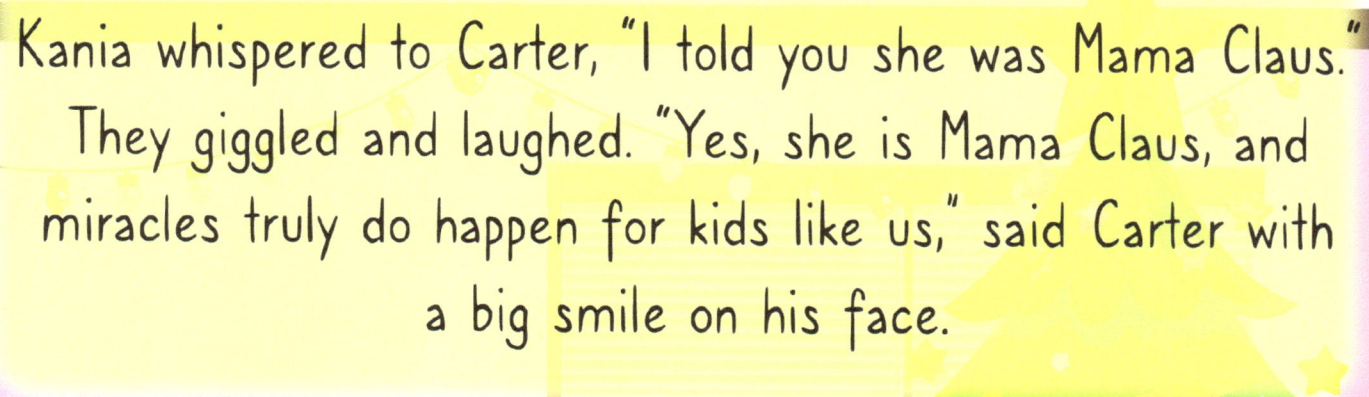

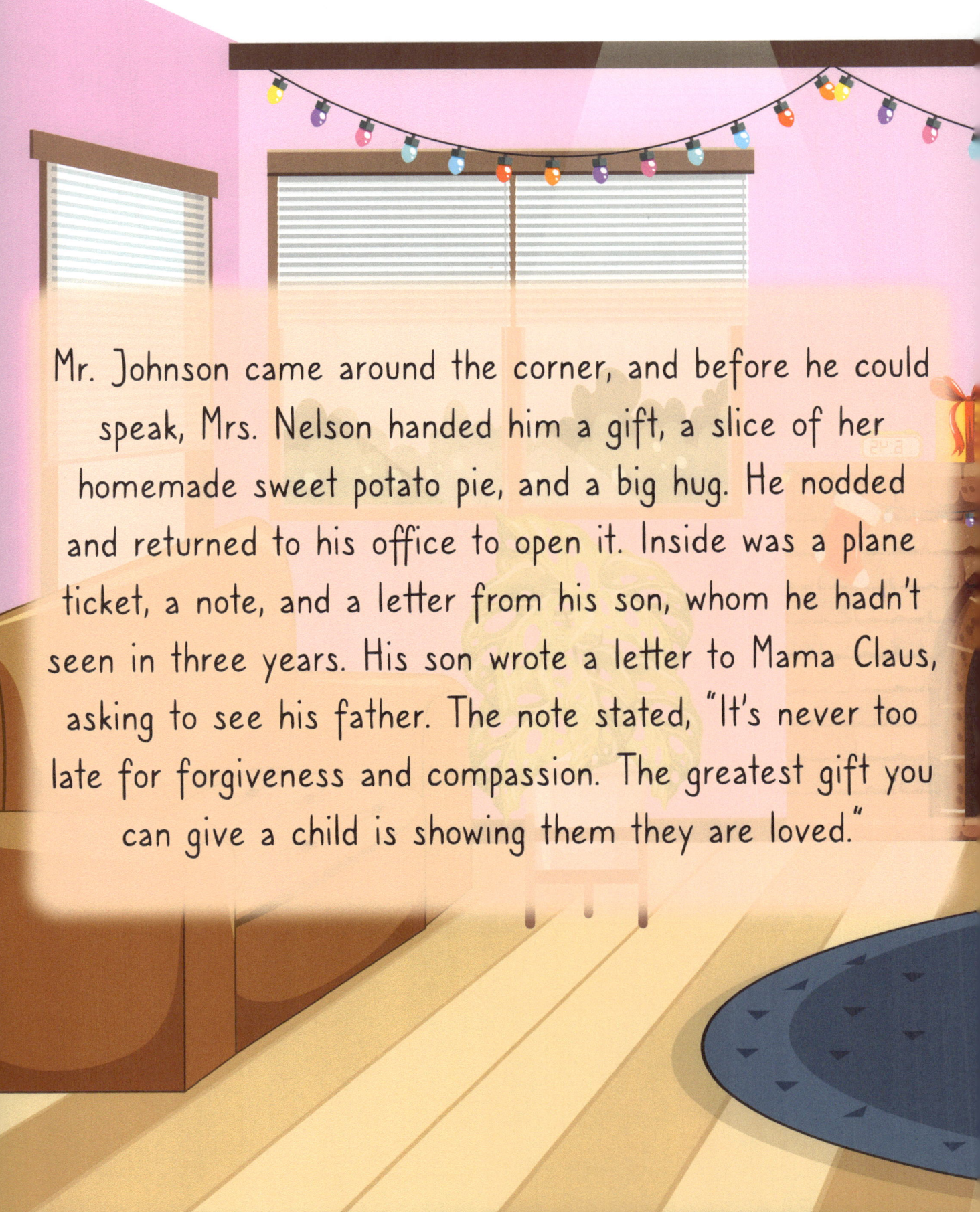

Mr. Johnson came around the corner, and before he could speak, Mrs. Nelson handed him a gift, a slice of her homemade sweet potato pie, and a big hug. He nodded and returned to his office to open it. Inside was a plane ticket, a note, and a letter from his son, whom he hadn't seen in three years. His son wrote a letter to Mama Claus, asking to see his father. The note stated, "It's never too late for forgiveness and compassion. The greatest gift you can give a child is showing them they are loved."

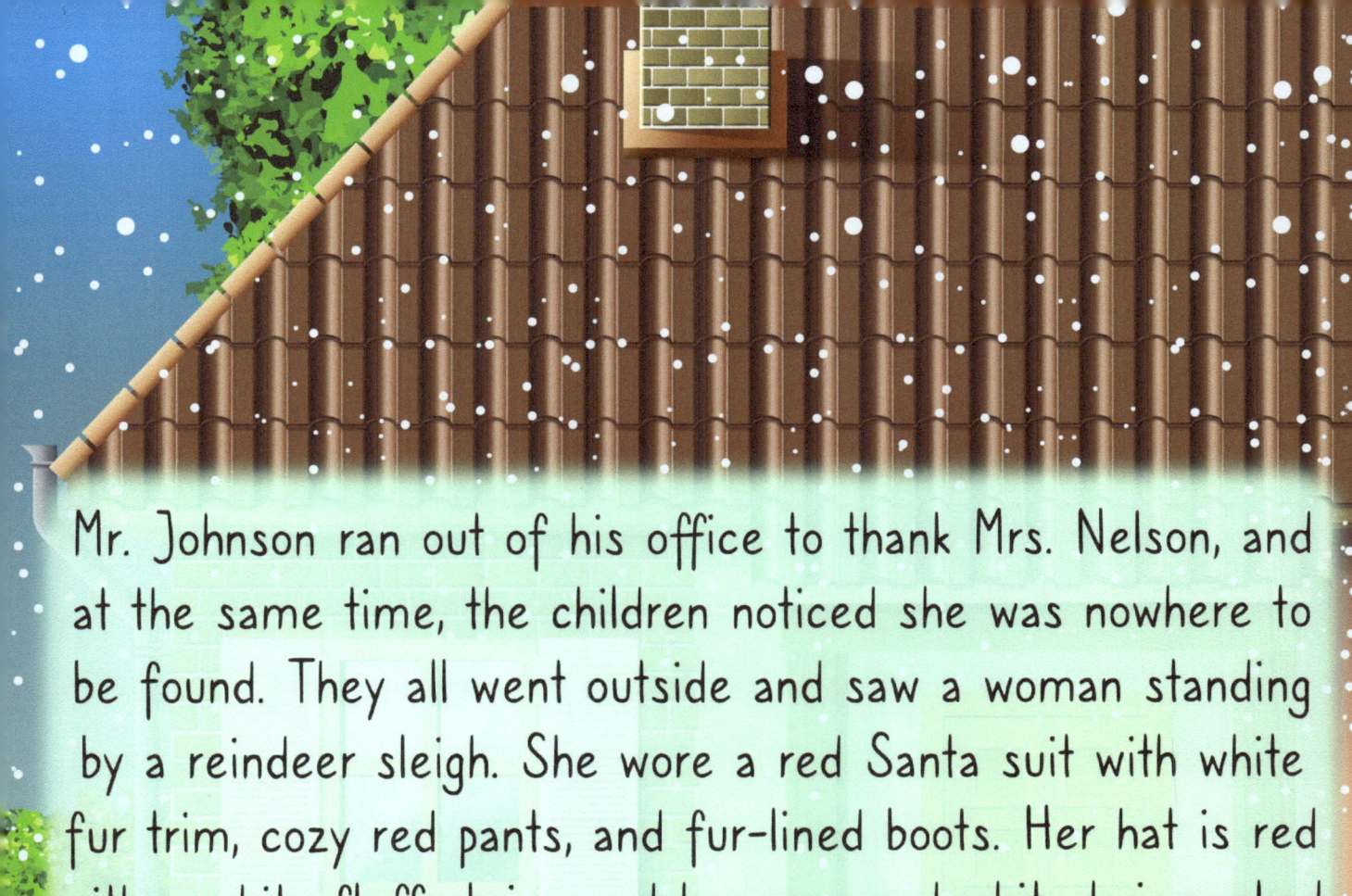

Mr. Johnson ran out of his office to thank Mrs. Nelson, and at the same time, the children noticed she was nowhere to be found. They all went outside and saw a woman standing by a reindeer sleigh. She wore a red Santa suit with white fur trim, cozy red pants, and fur-lined boots. Her hat is red with a white fluffy brim, and her grey and white hair peeked out in soft curls. She wore round glasses on her nose, adding to her grandmotherly charm. She had rosy cheeks as red as plums; and a gentle smile that makes everyone feel loved.

"Mrs. Nelson is Mama Claus!" Mr. Johnson said. The children looked at him in awe!! "Merry Christmas, and remember, everyone deserves to be loved," Mama Claus shouted as she rode off in her sleigh. And so, in the small town of Sumter, the legend of Mama Claus lived on, reminding everyone that kindness, love, and a little bit of Christmas magic can change lives forever.